Comp.

KEVIN DAVIES

EDGE

Parts of this work previously appeared in *Bivouac*; *Boo*; *The Exact Change Yearbook*; *The Imprecipient*; *Lingo*; *Object*; *On Your Knees, Citizen*; *Open Letter*; *Philly Talks*; and *Raddle Moon*. The sequence from pages 60 to 72 was issued as *Thunk* by Situations (New York, 1995). A few pages began their careers as collaborations with Abigail Child, Jeff Hull, and Andrea Mastor. Karnal bunt is a grain mould at the heart of a recent Canada–U.S. trade dispute.

The author wishes to thank Bruce Andrews, Deirdre Kovac, and Rod Smith for their keen editorial insights.

Cover image, design, and typesetting by Deirdre Kovac.

Edge Books are published by *Aerial* magazine.

Distributed by Small Press Distribution, Berkeley, CA
1-800-869-7553
orders@spdbooks.org

ISBN: 1-890311-08-1

Edge Books
P.O. Box 25642
Washington, D.C. 20007

aerialedge@aol.com

Comp.

What gets *me* is

　　　　　　　　the robots are doing
　　　my job, but I don't get
　　　　　　the *money*,
　　　some extrapolated node
　　　　　　　of expansion-contraction gets
　　　my money, which *I* need
　　　　　　for *time travel*.

Contents

1

Apocryphon

If you don't believe a science, don't misquote it

Just keep staring into that English-language night sky.

The entire panoply of minimalist histrionics.

Irish symptom frock

Doubt, as practice, a real symptom
of the imaginary death-throes of romanticism.

Let all these autobiographies do their own driving.

Be seeds a bird
guards.

In any writing that is actually an elephants' graveyard,

Gymnastic sarcasm of personality disintegration. Smell selves in puddles

                                        Polemical, a seance

To recur as a problem for theoretical kinesiology.

                    Do we imagine a wall
of children lurking behind support plinths?

                    Playgrounds and their equipment
recur as motif

Boulders since ground down to gravel.

A retired divine
Having tutored.

Eros
and Thanatos bobbing
for resemblance amidst
variously
severed bassoons.

That's
what it says
here.

I fall up
on the thorns of life,
I read

Repeat after
a player piano.

Internal refried social
nonfiction.

Many parts
of the distribution apparatus are
edible.

A true-to-life bucket of water thrown onto the obliviousness of the horse meter.

To substitute a chemically induced confidence for analysis
of what really makes the hypnotized dog-team go.

The obvious conclusion is deleted and replaced by footage of cross-border
    hooliganism recorded by a Bellingham TV reporter prior to the liberation
    of Ho Chi Minh City.

                         Stupendous
verbal neutrinos pass through all
anointed celebrants

                         Will migrate
A new country stuttering
out an invented documentary tradition

                              Or

why is this traffic speeding
up, toward what burning of what
holiday greens

I scraped and I painted till I bled blood
red on the flat black.
Then I stopped.
It is a cry for help!

We were brought to this world to advance the plot
Dad always said

                    A net

descends on the strategic hamlet. Treason

The immensity of the reams
placing
us, an excellent
and versatile condiment, always here
in an atmosphere
of previous tonnage, former clearance.

You get to be different by changing your "handwriting"
when supplying "samples"
to possible "employers."

To slow down
or turn tail
when approaching the roadblock.

But not if it means "behaving
to"
the groceries.

The different means of
imagining growth amongst the mutagens

Bulbous, diffident ancestors asked skies
for direction, now

Any sense
of completion is
invited in like
Any sense of depletion.

Lichen's one living example and moss another

walking off cliffs clutching peace dividends.

To offer up complication
is to betray the seamless curtain
of class somnolence

and

All memory false. Audibles called

at the line produce catastrophe

or last-minute victory (indistinguishable).

Belatedly protected habitats are picturesque.

The local archivist reduced to microfilmic speck

More powerful than fragments
of journal scratched on unorthodox surfaces
of private ownership, mere powder

strategic bankruptcies . . .

"I counsel you to walk right up to your foreman and spit."

By standing at the edge and peering in, we influence development.
Sleep, "a pitiful charade."

Age is wasted on the old. In love
with the distant prospect of dysfunction
the poverty coheres in series.
To have been a fountain

The relevant two classes emerging from the new
partnership of abridged matter invisible in the mirror.

Famous
                              educational
                                                              toggles.

You misunderstand — I'm *tasting* the

outside of the envelope. Forget this

testing business — that's *school*.

        A series of twelve-minute health kicks spread out over a decade of cloud
and spatulas.
        The circus having run away with the only part of him with a hope of
becoming a cactus.
        The music keeps thumping
        "because the whole world needs thumping." A text-
        book case of unintentional toddler
        siblings, vanguard trash-
        heap tempi,
        four bars beyond the improvisation

Sequential thought quota.   Hare-brained dirigible regulation

as one with the moat in your passion,
most Albigensian of all my friends.
Recognize the drift of acid snow the words
are lodged in. Enough natter's
going on-line to fritz-out the drawbridge. Heresy
a deep image, in a field of cast-off Dictaphones . . .

A made world
lying in the weight of perjured foster care

      The main difference between me and my shadow is *I am* the more
disciplined smoker

      and when I hear the words "second coming" I grab my Manlicher-
Corricano and go looking for a book depository.

Young
dead
neoliberalism.

Class chasm of Hazlitt's passion

For years
a kind of conceptual art too ephemeral to be documented

I am in your debt, oh loggerhead

                      of instinctual unnesting.

. . . cheapened by mere proximity . . .

If it's not too late I have a few questions

What is "pit-lamping Nazi skins" an action or a description

If I had a camera would I be allowed to walk around

Human beings are definitely alligators correct?

Violence, vulgarity, adult situations.

Everything is going on
at length, almost every day now

                          B Train D Train F Train

This reverence, this irreverence, these car alarms

                    Fair Play for Cuba

We'll embargo the universal health care out of their literate Third World butts

Those potential

                                             Florida Republicans

Memories of overdevelopment

        Words in the process of becoming cash crops. Verbal
exhaustion trying to stand in for millennia of solar-eclipse data hoarded by
        the priestly caste. Wards of the statement — hunkering, predicated.
Uncles and aunts driving away to charges later reduced to booze-induced
        melancholy. Port Babel, Ether Ridge, Extreme Junction,
Jackmormon Creek, Chumleyville, Them-Birds.
        The kind of tough, stringy, and foul-tasting duck a sea gull
makes at table in the postwar DP forties, learning rope

        Actually *buying soap* at the drug bodega

The posthumous jukebox of passion plays what *it* wants

        in a sandbox, the buckets of it

I am dancing on your table because, I love you

        Now divided

You know who you were

        You knew who you are

all popped like kernels

Documentary precedes epic

Class enemies eaten during Cultural Revolution

Monster hit of ego vapours

Self-replicating soccer pitches lost in space

Drone, cackle, threnody, duct tape, expression, pasta, glaze, the skull
bones of snipers

Yes thanks
for the warning,
put it in writing,
see you later.

A pugnacity that is its own reward
Its sewn seed repeated as memoir

Not so much

held together and standing firm as braced apart and stunned by the sideshow

We are getting very sleepy
There's a hum coming from the metacorporate world-ruler thing-dinger

Post-social

Vivisectional

Distribution.

Of all the substances humans have contrived to alter consciousness
This,
This is the most devout and repetitive
This,
This is the most devout and repetitive
It is a new life of world-assembling impetuosities
Alone and in company
It is the late day of a month in a year
— Spotted owls, get in line
Spotted-owl crowd, get in line —
The rerun of the oppressed

We have to stop them
sandblasting the bridge dirt
into our blood face.

Roof access and
weather, a sense of parades having happened to pass.

A flabbergasted A-student type.

You can more or less count on being part of the control group.

Five Poems Employing
Jackson Mac Low's "Daily Life"
Procedure, with Variations on
the Letter *U*, July 1997
(titles decayed)

1.

The Id-driven anti-oater of cinematic latency.
Rubbing.
Stand there holding this award against the surface of history.
At home between the ceiling and the crawlspace.
Here, the society for nonnarrative municipal government.

Variations in domestic sky.
This we translate "give me the cash; ignore the container."
My bones seek Nixon in the cloakroom.
The point, however, is to change *it*.
Stand there holding this award against the surface of history.
For only school is real.

Class violence at the level of the seedling.
Anselm's fisting Cheetos.
Right now, before they abolish welfare or something.
My bones seek Nixon in the cloakroom.
Hand me the Bulgarian umbrella, comrade.
The Id-driven anti-Oater of cinematic latency.
The big secret.

2.

The little secret.
This we translate "vernacular hell of feedbag negotiation."
The point, however, is to change *it*.
The general goo between them.

Convicted tutor.
The Id-driven anti-Oater of cinematic latency.
Self-employed as the day is logged off.
Anselm's fisting Cheetos.
This we translate "for example, 'taming the monkey mind.'"
Here, the society for nonnarrative municipal government.

3.

At home between the ceiling and the crawlspace.
Several idiots dynamiting a discourse outlet.
Stand there holding this award against the surface of history.
Here, the society for nonnarrative municipal government.
The Id-driven anti-Oater of cinematic latency.

Contradicted within the ludic embrace of such moments.
At home between the ceiling and the crawlspace.
The Id-driven anti-Oater of cinematic latency.
Here, the society for nonnarrative municipal government.
Organisms wander off.
For only school is real.

At home between the ceiling and the crawlspace.
The big secret.
Class violence at the level of the seedling.
The point, however, is to change *it*.
The big secret.
At home between the ceiling and the crawlspace.
Contradicted within the ludic embrace of such moments.

4.

The idea of the very compressed.
Anselm's fisting Cheetos.
Anselm's fisting Cheetos.
The idea of the very compressed.

A drone across vast Gowanus.
The point, however, is to change *it*.
Stand there holding this award against the surface of history.
At home between the ceiling and the crawlspace.
Contradicted within the ludic embrace of such moments.

These are examples of the lozenges our factory produces.
Anselm's fisting Cheetos.
This we translate "folded arms of the mother robot."
The big secret.
Class violence at the level of the seedling.

Dream of interminable Vole reunion tour.
Anselm's fisting Cheetos.
Here, the society for nonnarrative municipal government.
The idea of the very compressed.
At home between the ceiling and the crawlspace.
Here, the society for nonnarrative municipal government.

5.

Right now, before they abolish welfare or something.
This we translate "seventeen rainboat enriched uranium hut-hut."
Several idiots dynamiting a discourse outlet.
The little secret.
This we translate "'keypop hamper.'"
At home between the ceiling and the crawlspace.
A drone across vast Gowanus.

The general goo between them.
This we translate "omnibus trade bill."
A drone across vast Gowanus.
Right now, before they abolish welfare or something.
The point, however, is to change *it*.
The general goo between them.
Organisms wander off.

25

Karnal Bunt

•

Cosmic junk fish or something.

The comedy of the paragraph of the landscape of the hunger of it.

The American Dream's a pyramid scheme, reborn every minute.

Years of training,

will there ever be an end to these flashcards?

I would *gladly* trade bodies

Will fuck for books, no weirdoes

Lions, Tigers, Bears, Disjunction, Curtains on fire
The pleasures of the whip in autumn

.

If the dream is of China, of working
along the seacoast of a China, within
ambiguous class relations
on a commuter train, in China, therefore.

Water keeps recurring in these
little captains.

Never ignore a protein source or
no complaining if you do.

A familiar ballpark
figure.

•

To wallow in the thought
of a return
to Capistrano, an exact science
of knowing
how and where
to read
all about it.
Archaic monks and
maidens splayed
upon chairs on lawns, waiting
to be violated
by our fin-de-siècle
insouciance, the planks
of our new party's platform
heels, pieces
of period, whirling on axes.

•

                Lovers walk
the seawall of this scratch-and-sniff principality
                        what am I bid and so on but
        that's lame —

        Serendipitous art
                    of incompetent drop cap
        Elaborate heart of incontinent
              fry cook

                Libraries
      of ego communism
      Stalwart the conjunction of rivers comrade

        Bring your pasta Sacramento to the potluck
        Bring the toys

•

Rock, butts, brick, limbs, little bits of park.
Without whose municipal grace   "Doctor, let me die." *(Exit left.)*

      (1) These water towers
weren't constructed by space
aliens. (2) Every rich country
has emergency martial-law plans
and functionaries eager to try them out.
(3) Every large corporation
has a spy network.   Right?

      (4) That's where we come in.   Right?

      (5) We can't understand each other
through our particle masks.   Right?

      (6) Or we expect an anchoring effect to take
hold beyond a certain
durational boundary.   *Right?*

      (7) There's nothing certain
about it. (8) The ridicule we splatter on
our virtual selves has a destination
past its target. (9) I pity you, man. (10) Everything's
beyond this moment but
it's all here. (11) The acoustics
are shocking. (12) That's why we stand puzzled before elevator
shafts, all alone.   Right? (13) But

         Mistakes are sexual.

         Stroke my residency permit.

•

My heart — the one I never
learned to notate — flips
flapjacks in the trailer camp
of a Yellowknife gold mine.
It doesn't know why.
And if I want to feel
good all over again
I give up
and feel good giving up
all over again.
No he said probably the guy
is changed somehow for the better or
worse, or dies or,
is blackmailed. Because if
it's an experiment who's
monitoring? Or maybe he's
a woman. *I* don't know.
Was the details in the middle that
interested him or her.
Easier to fill out a form that's already replaced you. Information
wants to be me. O
K.

                                                    Inept tennis
                                                    and vice versa.

Useful to imagine yourself a satellite, but eventually you've got to cut it out. A
ghosted town, broken shutters battering barrels. You pictured it you bought it.
You burned it down you *gotta* sweep it up. Jan always buzzed we aren't the only
non sequiturs in this fish plant honey.

•

Quote Yeah you *wish* my abandoned command post were closer to your
retrieval plant and wholly owned subsidiaries. You *want* the polka dots to be
Aristotelian. Couldn't beadle my furrows evangelistically enough for you
could I, yeah baby I know it hurts. I know because *I went to Fredericton and stayed
there*, I painted baseboards vermilion for dunce dimes and ninny nickels.
That doesn't mean I have to waddle up to raccoon-juice-cooled marsh elders
with alder awnings and slant-six Norwegian method acting strapped to
their fungoes to know when I'm not connecting the weather bucket to the wet
side of the post-minimalism. I know when I'm not hunted. Just don't
expect lemurs to magically reappear from the fine print of the self-storage
contract. Don't even *think* about viola solos. We all just re-upped with the
radiator fuzz Un Quote.

I learned the year after kindergarten that sentences
are linguistic artifacts with regulations that fill them-
selves out, and that for the purposes of our circus-cannon
ambitions the most important part of the war they enact
is the full-stopping dots that divide the booty amongst
camp-following berzerkers of the sub-syllabic frontier. Word.

•

It
has a theme, like
all serious
works of art,
and is meaningless,
and its cuffs,
newly flared
in parody of
historicism's fatuities,
drag
across living mud.

                              Fear flips out

                        in the on-deck circle

              Mahler lieder stun dart
                    thirst.

              Squeaky bent rims of psycho-
                    tropic aquarium grit

      game. Knock knock

                              knockin on.

•

You win the game by advancing to "Summer Vacation" ("Death" in the original
    Irish version) without having to share any of your misappropriations.

Jars
of telekinetic parricide. A January. A sort
of type, a list

of careers that
hum.
A tradition, chopping its own wood

Once a year, a halter, pumps, stockings with garter, tight red skirt, a little
    mascara, all alone with the light from another room, phoning everyone
    you know and hanging up after one ring, this is mandatory if you want to
    continue in the program, call it a *required rereading* course, it's not a soft
    option like Intentional Dehydration or Reciting Shelley's End-Rhymes
    Upwards While Sneezing or Leaving Fudge for the Letter Carrier or
    Replacing All Your Condiments with Pictures of Where You Figure They
    Come From or Voicing Vocational Doubts to War-Memorial Retaining
    Walls Where Spivs Loiter in Towns the Train Stopped Stopping At. For
    extra credit dangle pee-wee forms of former demons off the tip of
    extended foot resting on whatever object stands in for what you call an
    ottoman before flicking them off into unlit linoleum abyss.

                            Political, a science.

———

•

Humans
illustrating their own goals,
giving frustrated
slide shows, knowing something
        —Who *are* they?
whose platitudinous résumés begin
so hopefully, whose distinguishing
features float free
and enlarge in caricature, *us? No way!*

Wealth
A tonsured vocalist
dumping oranges in the harbour.

            despite pit-lamp shit-scoop employment loop

            become fucked in ass for once of universe

•

Preposterous vacillation at the foul line.

From death-haunted provincial to rootless, down-at-heels cosmopolite in
    numberless steps

                          jokes.

No better than donkeys
                              bulldozed off cliffs in the sequel

Whole ideological technologies proposed

And abandoned amidst the happy clog dancing our presences aspire to.

•

The consolation of a rich
outer life, accentuated, made
poignant by, a government-
sponsored sleep-deprivation
program integrated with
the consolidation of stray facts
into fully erect
adult earning power, gated and patrolled.

quotable thought sequence

If we doubted our function
we'd immediately go out.   But

•

Entranced by examples
of municipal order gone wrong
and zombie burghers' cars that talk back to transience

For which the old words are
remedial life and
denatured maniac liaison blockage.
Images beehiving in a comedy of air horns.
An exception
at which we sit
becoming unwashed.

An edited Scotch ambiance of translated Chinese reads to itself.

•

In that sense it's still anybody's meaningless post-Series tour of the new Axis alliance.

Evangelical 24-second clock.

More concerned about personal stats than team glory.

Even Agnew refused to wrestle kangaroos for money. Pitbull slays spaniel while owners watch weeping in a poem Silliman won't write till three May Days after the assassination of Lyndon Larouche. Flub grammar to put illiterate MBAs at ease. That's how I became Mr. Tax Crank, and Mr. Elevator Consultant, and the Right Reverend Monsignor Lucas Frisbee. I happen to like the way Chretién's partial facial paralysis causes him to speak, but that's it, end of file. So what did that pundit mean by "nominally heterosexual" and what unrepeatably complex set of impulses and POV shots did it attempt to syndicate? These people we used to be are shed skins more hangdog than the day after election day mumbling into broken microphones and picking at residual glue of expired expiry-date stickers. You, actually believe that? You wanna go out for the possibility of ecstatic reverb or order-in the chance of transforming enlightenment? Leaders of the corporate pod grow weary in their birthday leathers, drinking deep from the sabotaged cooler and later dictating glossolaliac memos before suiciding in traffic tunnels. Neural stilt-walkers of the friendly apocalypse, howdy! Their boyfriends, hello! Codependents, welcome!

•

That which listens to hiss, the this
occipital chafing, tinnitic Rorschach
        Tourette's. Everyone's got their
fucking story eh. This city-
        fucking-zenship.

No barrier that is not a lingering talent.

•

That all fates are thus in this mountain universe!

Shivering

Venereal

Ascension.

                              I like the feel of experiencing myself
                              making a decision that is itself deciding
                              to experience the feel of welcome in me.

                    That peppers might grow, and bats find crannies.

Passports glowing like gnosis in the crawl space

•

Quieten: the parapsychological realism
can't hear itself speak my thoughts.

There's no clue. To be clueless
is to experience unconscious languor, a bonus.

That's called
Brief fantasy.   *lunar dentistry*

so what's the problem. You like
to imagine being held down by astronauts.

Doesn't fit with what you otherwise control of your mandate.

If you have decks, clear them.
If you are with boom, lower it
in successive freeze-frames down
till it is just another uncontested
orphan in a salt lake of others.

Tried it in the sixties and never exhaled.

"Hey Man" and the unthought are drinking buddies.

To become unhinged is to admit, finally, the existence of hinges.

All members of society contain feathers.

•

Two years undercover as a transvestite hooker giving head to mob slabs and bent cops, now you're telling me it was all a practical joke?

Language isn't not not neutral and so on.

I want the dharma *now* without having to work for it or actually becoming a Buddhist.

This, once a pillar of a temple of Minerva, now the business section of a Maryland daily, replaces what I might have thought with the Will to Be a Thought, an Impulse in an Overmind, Vaster than the Bellowing of Church League Lacrosse.

Unlike the watched pot, which does eventually boil, if you scan yourself for signs of becoming a Bodhisattva you'll never be one. Haldeman knew this but couldn't accept it.

———

•

In faxed cul-de-sacs of postindustrial cheater's guides of stray pop glossed

Panhandlers get quarters to continue.

Every false note betrays the breeding of its parent structure.
The grasses have plot complications written on their wild cultures.

I admire a drug that allows you to hear and feel the
empty husks of brain cells landing on the
lodgings of evicted homunculi.

Imaginary lines circle planet, intersecting Sisyphean religiosity.

If you want the manual you've got to buy the program.

•

My youngishness
responds to the explanatory
mode! Had thought
had happily lost
self in endless clauses
of sentence but
the period lurked, a re-
integrating terminus bitter
as a diet of aluminum. We

A pheasant and a bugle
in a field by a scholar.

had to shoot
them, or be
shot ourselves.
This trial is a farce!

•

Ramshackledness of assumed persona is/equals 'lude tones of news
foods. Quote we will kick their cracker asses. Domes. Pirate radio launched
over handlebars of already decayed bad-hair decade. The craft to such
rough outlines in the air of an afternoon in somewhere, rewound and repeated,
gaining solidity and permanence with constant viewing, unedited
evidence of constant viewing. Nature as grave, as opposed to nature as language
game, as opposed to nature as lathe, as opposed to local ordinance. You
are why you eat.

•

Gravy?   More a soup

If gestural, if festive epic material, if pre-mechanical, if prone, if
backdrop marginalia

festooned

Acting normal as a kind of overfunded performance art kids are encouraged to
express themselves with.

For all the theoretical possibilities of life, the same chimney keeps toppling in
the same movie and

the same cherry trees mate across distances, anxious about their welcome.

As good as it got — Imaginary
yet viable, displaying social intentions —

Which, when burned, made light —

•

I apply for work
                in the War Room.

Friends aren't art and can't read.

        Tragic life, drunkenness, religious mania, these
four last songs — Fish jump at the periphery of the chorus — Unflinching
in their adherence to democratic centralism, fast forward —

I'm propped against
a tree I didn't plant,
a tentacle-held paradigm that is the
policy of our organ.

                                Why be sad?
                                Kissinger will die
                                before they can upload him.

Yet
            what if there's a perfectly natural
form, and god wants us to kiss it and talk dirty?

•

Various

               daybreak

                              spermatozoa.

I took to the woods with a camp kit and a stack of Patricia Highsmith novels
    but couldn't hack it and got a room in a town down the coast and dug in
    long enough to be quizzed by a couple of Junior Kiwanis types which led
    me to give notice at the mortuary and use the accumulated vacation pay to
    buy a newish pocket flügelhorn to flee across the continent with and learn
    to play

For instance, you might wish to be simpler
but be dissatisfied when wish is granted. Or
I might grate against the puny volume I
suck in, but expand me and "I" breaks. Similarly, . . .

•

China Cat,

Body Bag, smudged

war-mongering matter
settling into constituent boroughs
naked before community-access
television

So much confidence, so many boatless rudders

I will hold well this boom mike high above the heads of the speakers.

It is not tuberculosis that is the topic, but the manner by which its
    extrapulmonary class specifics become audible.

●

Ridiculous
landlocked miasma, let me get you a sweater.

Sentences
are acceptable only insofar as they can be translated into Latin
with their meanings intact and confidence in empire unimpaired.

Never
apologize, never send thank-you notes.

Persons
atop the peak of your life, claiming it for England.

Curiosity
pieces itself together between acts
of familial treachery, this is normal.

•

    The desire to hide is *rational* — We're *made* of the bits the nineteenth century lopped off — But this is a *great* time for vegetables — Alcohol is *pedantic* — *You* know, the fact that we're ruled by the money that owns the people who have the money that rules itself — The *nitwit* at the heart of the world-heart — Sabotage is your *duty* — Entropy is *built* into the chicken —

Spoken by Jeff Hull in a dream:

Move around some Get that anarcho-recidivism slinking through the hardware
    Interruption

Itself becomes narrative Bathtub farts are theory panels Rent a car The art part

Of the battered brain Staten Island out of New York State America out of Milky
    Way now!

•

I love the look of humans when they sit or stand still and when they move around

I love the look of them looking back and barking arbitrary commands, which I
obey

I love the fragrance of the grouping of incommensurate ego fantasias in the
drone of winter

I love the fuss of the not-quite of submission techniques

I love to be an international unit in the measure of the loading of the fissures in
the communal membrane into silos on a prairie in a basement by a
government of souls in trouble at a party with martinis for a long time

Total sodomy.

•

And as for the psycho-socio trance

of art armies massing

on the frontiers of what love laughs at and vice versa . . .

Sexually attracted to the bandaged
Sexually attracted to the head-wound type.
Sexually attracted to the bandaged

.

Linguistics — whoops —wrong horse

It is necessary to fracture the logics of identity
without however becoming a burden on one's friends.

It is useful to raise welts on the unconscious hide
of metaphor, so that we can have fun.

It is important to get on television and stay there.

An irrepressible gee-gawism, collectors' edition
subsistence rations, steal a job, give the gift of dick-enlargement surgery, keep
voting —

I choose to be pregnant with gay triplets

Genital resonance.

•

Learning from Los Alamos.
The brain was saved for later.
Leaning into Los Angeles.
Leaping onto the back of the senatorial beast.

a pedestrian clairvoyance

ratted-on by automotive predestination

in a Disneyed line-item plutocracy and

onward.

nimbly to vacate the nameplate and eat the key

•

I'm weak on history's

        particulates and generosities

                The exile of ectoplasmic humanity

so derived from divisions of its force —

The organization
of these petals in a crowd of echoes in
a tunnel. The trailer
that precedes the feature
in the polycentric theatre of the nonfuture.

Money tends to inherit itself.

•

I would love to lie here and concentrate on this Portuguese music to the
    exclusion of much else

The way that it is right and wrong and ongoing, the decals that adhere to its
    glamour

Such sounds as quicken me to the very marrow of the vampiric electoral
    college I host

                                        The precepts of materialism
interrogated by their own kittenish desires . . .

Nothing rhymes with this job.

                              N Train R Train.

                                        Was Schoenberg ever *not* pissed off?

•

'Cause blues go, get lost on
        soft roofs of
the next thoughts that drop off the Taylorized rope bridge across our *candours* —

Charisma of morning oxygen,
            totally numb with vista.

        An unparalleled and
very nervous breakdown of underground
Mirror Doors.

                    "I knew I was a formal device
                    before I was born. I wanted
                    a *bigger* prize, for having survived."

•

The sharecropper catastrophe
and suicide moth on-
purpose garden borders of human
affinity groups. More
microclimatic cow-
kicked alarm clocks.
The differently flooded Methodism. A shed.

•

There's nothing superficial about the way all that stuff burrows into any
    available crack

in the sidewalk, growing back, covering, by logical extension if not in fact,
    everything.

Every junked
vehicle a
proposition
waiting for
the right rustic
welder
after the war that
never happened
here.

> Parts
of the body can't
> get interested in
these computer details
> break.
> Semi-derelict
together signaling.
> If you can't laugh
don't spasm
> and live together.
> Those words
in mind are
> lamblike and
enthusiastic fishers.
> Who has a yacht
might wander.
> If you can't wash
don't doctor.

•

Can't speak for you, but when I host palpitations I quit talking for a day,
     communicating with only the signals a catcher commonly flashes with a
     runner on second.

Getting position under the hoop does not require height, weight, or even
     existence as we now understand it.

•

There can be no authenticating misdemeanour without the Zeno-like transaction of sheer expectation edging up the spine of a term whose number is any but

four — or, say, not a burned rube but a virtual divot, propelled in an arc over economies projected by double-blind research and

down, down upon the jittery picnic of witness protection.

•

From each according to the vituperative whiplash of each understanding, to each according to the brazenness of each exotic toe, elongated and erectile in a state-withered world of contemplative dalliance. VIVA CLASS HATE! Rules? We'll look back some day from the apex of the jet-pack trajectory and recognize the mannerism for what's opaque of its method, be measured by its upward regard of our proclivities, as lost to each other as toast to breakfast on the '86 death shuttle. Coin on string in human holes. Débris plucked from landfill placed perhaps as offering on futon — END TRANSMISSION —

•

Hometowns are *reformist idiots*.

•

Unauthorized military decapitation in Germany. Surfin
bio-chem Nobel-getter doubts HIV makes AIDS. Clinton
licks tender inner thigh of corporate crud agenda. Mass
bust of pan-ethnic smack gang leaves streets greasy with
fear schemes. Compromise candidate rejects proffered
straw stuffing, stutter-steps past honour guard and trades
sceptre for puerile pottage on forever bender. Final
arguments continue.

And swear by the
intelligence
of my middle
lip to describe
the entrails of the prophesy and
anticipate
the wooden hat.

These cheesy little hypertexts
are going to get better.
I don't know
how *much* better, but *we'll see*.

•

An antipersonnel erotic
encrypted by the autodidact
via anapestic solos in a
baritone of stairwell welfare.

When I am in my emphysema
a ferry is as though departing in the dark toward a saga
and lectures are landfill an art of Manhattan an ozone alert and a promise.

Quit naming the animals

·

(Brahmsian wetlands)

·

Astral rot and shining poultry.
Instruction falling, from parted beams
to declivities of luckless macho.

A decade on the shore of some fable
knotting a tie.
And here I am
after wrap, ripped on Cary's secret stash,
astride a friendly stranger's moped having fun forever, bye!

•

The thrill of being misquoted, of inserting miniature cars in the urethra

I'm sorry, but I don't speak Russian.

They look like

Emergency fire exits but actually

They're weapons.

•

I don't find this funny and am heartened

An end-of-millennium German libretto

What a fabulous
            continuation of sculpture by other means!

Brick by sexual machine tourist
In bed with the neighbourhood

.

                    Flying into the handle,
              raised up variously for our pelts and flesh

The law.

One having become bored
by the other and the other become numb
to the imagining of the one

So, let's get together and exchange goods.
Sixty years later the park is closed to correct the original design flaws.
I saw the three previous versions including the silent.

•

I have more or less exhaled this romance

Corrupt as Rhode Island politics

Less visible to the touristed *enabler* than a burnt and buried map of Tajikistan in
crisis

Monocultural

Lysenkoist

Phrenologies.

·

. . . farewell, and good luck with the insurance fraud schemes,
don't let your zombie master learn your new number,
live for love . . .

•

That pleasure lent from these ends of instructibility,
the expansion of the universe, and the hypothesized existence of language
to lives that are conceived as such, ongoing,
reflected, moved, and fucked, pausing now, buzzed, getting down.

Phobic
nook, proletarian character bed, rank with rented Free World prototypes, golf
course pork medallions.

Anonymity breeds content.

You get what you get, in time.
Are got at.
We're willed to the guesswork
of event, the eventual
abstract, a blurring of madrigals.
A pledge is a principle of physics.

Translation: Croppies lie down.

•

Speaking
as a fingerprinted alien
a feasting wedge of antimatter in socks and shoes

Butch feels better after dialysis
though he's angry Andrea hired Tony to shovel snow.
Cookie needs two dollars and forty cents for crack.

All this will have to be radically cut back to save the suburbs.

•

Prolife shutterbugs
amongst the dahlias of their reward

The assassination of Pinochet as he stands gobbing into lily pond

Blank

Pathos a stretch fabric in the gap of utterance

So,
I think you think doubt is childish
Embargoed cigars in the foreground
The problem with one-party American democracy is its obnoxious dream life
Knotted into public adjectives, polluting the water table
Scratching its ass on the lens of the camcorder while passing sentence. Doubt

it.

Pathos a stretch fabric.

The tracking of haywire manatees . . .

An unstartled auditor can't replicate. Is that
it? The Buddha died horribly, food poisoning or bad water.
He was an old duffer with hangers-on.
I've never been able to make sense of the glosses.

•

Welfare recipients as potential scab force

The completion of modernity, the washing up, the beers after

A small or
large machine made of birds

        jailed by

pentagons of reversible terms, collapsed amidst the globalized clearcut

Endophasia   a device for accelerating protons

That's what happens when you give a community of teenagers a truckload of
        pixelvision and tell it to start shooting.

Squamiform

•

Drafty, blowhard world. Is nuts
to cheekbones of animal ratio.

Easier just to keep working than it ever is to stop.

A flat tax.

The noted social anthropologist.

I'm comfortable with my attention span.

To become a mere episode
in the history of indoor compost is to reclaim a garden
in the craters of chronology.
Dogs upon a narrative marsh . . .

I can't think without devils!

•

Cling to these strangers
Dreams of compulsive face scrubbing
Toxic, out-of-work canals are lovely

You are getting very sleepy, the next time a siren sounds you will bite off
all your fingers, mail them to me c/o the Graduate Student Lounge, Duane State
University, Duane, Tennessee (*not* the Rushmore campus) . . .

Break a stick and there I am —   capitalism

We used to say, an earth-orbiting dowager empress
Distributed around the command module with sound and picture
Turned off and the kettle boiling

———

81

Untitled Poem from the First Clinton Administration

Monster of agricultural division

                          go forth,

Landlord and tenant,

                    undergrad and lab rat

An unfunded social wish list, urban job jar

Five hours upriver on the border near the moon

Colloquial variant

Colombia own-goal nightclub execution

In the chewed margin of luxury

Because we are paid

In a way that sucks the queries from one's very pouch

Organs of corporeal whim

Said Ruskin, Hideous reply of human stew

Everything will be fine when you wake up, cool

Under the blinking satellites

And true in autumn to

The ownership of the means of reduction

Stars

Baked and trembling

Unknowing tool of the neo-feudal

Info order

Scratching in the airborne dirt of total eviction

From here in the bunker

All the radar blips look friendly and ambitious

Doug's again got

Air in his various balls

All thanks to the miracle of electrification

The recent hiring freeze

New canine breeds

The litter of domestic mist

One enormous vascular system

They had names once

Big piles of them in a slough between formations

Photographed by Martian tourists

These are my parents before they gave up

They can be represented mathematically as follows

I suspect them of having been agents
My heart is filled with hatred for all that exists
Berry-eating nomad battalions, larval solitude narration
Panic in the apiary
A little bit of lake gone critical within the blender
Gathered up into the arms of the redeemer
The last cigarette of the silly season

                                                                  Fog

                    Doubles

      Reason

                                      Woolly

                                        Thing-

                                                    Blanket

                    Crackhead

          Windows 95

                  A crony comes over and says the following
Stop being so obvious
When a new word enters the language
No, wait, I can't think, you're pressuring me
I know you are but what am I
Truncated gerund
But that doesn't count for shit
The fuck needs to have his head shoved in a trunk and thrown off a ship
And
I'd break your leg but I like your hair
Poxy stock jock
Yeah like entering a new century is about to change us into *Yellow Book* elves
Space-age chipmunks
Running for office
I don't even *play* tennis
Shoot me if
OK but
                  Serve
Serb artillery
I'm Andy Benes in Sarejevo
France bombs atoll

Dad always said it was a skank nation

Cal Ripkin shot dead one game short of record

Happy birthday John Cage

You were

            so unusual

You could've cleaned up in advertising

I figure

Zinc orbit

Obituary formalism

They don't care about the details but fuck with the structure and they'll crush
     your spine

A shell of other people

Reflowered

Pressed into action

Figures of demented nostalgia

With diplomas, credit histories

Unbridgeable gaps where their eyes should be

The cramp as such

Because it is written

Veins in the forearm of *Satan*

Like unanswered mail in a bag of doughnuts

The entire earth

Trembles in the throes of its decision-making process

Whole herds gobbled where they stand

A kiosk on a rocky ledge

A large vat of boiling ribbons

But cleverish end-of-history wads say nah

A serious civil right

There is no such thing as American poetry

Foreign concepts

Old school

Vast hick soup

Butted

Bent double

Moving these boxes up one more flight of stairs

A kind of sit-com clarity to the absolute mess of civilian life

Gone Sparta

Bonkers in Brooklyn

Part 2: Martini Summer

Filmed in Toronto standing in for Singapore

Whipped into shape by bank mergers bearding for the global theft of public
wealth

Personally is a good way to take it

Starlings at war with yellowjackets

The power of *Christ* compels you

Burned

Bunt single

Blank

The anger and ambition of international students

Their raw noses

Sniffing the park

Going on to reenactments, translations of certain moral fables

My heart racing against the image of an inlet

Thumps on the ceiling

Naked before the congregation

Walking the woods with a grandparent during the Kennedy administration

In another country

The details

Knees drawn up against nipples

Blasting the heads off the alien corn

Fried

Porked

Kersplatted

Reborn

De-boned

Tipped

Pleasure unending

Almost able to breathe

Hostages

Volunteers

Floating into the room like arrogant *geese*

Lenin getting a blowjob

On the way to the Finland Station
Just lean back
Now flip over
I can't even remember what you look like
Alive in the water
Meditating atop broken tractor parts
Not a pretty sight
Not an excuse for treachery
Not the same
Not the long light of evening
Not even beautiful unless placed against that outline
Not only fascinating but poisonous
Not structurally sound
Not not political
Not splendid
Not impossible
Not racy enough for current taste
Not built for speed
Not reversible due to judicial error
Not a page of monopoly news caught up by wind in a fence
Not the little animals that live almost unnoticed underneath the underground
Not the right analogy
Not the right time to be getting all maudlin
I'm going to say something to you students and then disappear
Your names have luggage
I wouldn't dream of allowing you to leave here alive
Not the appropriate comparison
My job is to suggest that the boilerplate sucks
But I want to be a liberal student
Of the art of war
Dressed well
Starving to death
Raised by *swans*
Dashed against holograms
Because the strain of living a lie becomes studded with the opals of minor
    aristocracy

Chinning my person
That's what's wrong with American education goddammit
Nobody has lips anymore
All everyone wants to do is rub money on their genitals
Hey I'm no exception
You get used to it
Actually it's not that bad
I'm training imaginary insects to eat away at my vocabulary
I just want to say a big hearty
Because why
Why but
But I
Cannot endorse the agenda
I'd do a little investigating into what batteries you're going to need
For complicated reasons
Even while the moneyless
Parasites of America are held down while a bipartisan congress takes shits in
    their mouths
For immigrants America is full of mysteries
Who to eat
Where to invest
Post-Fordist
The way I'd want to glower if I actually existed
Irritating like a hanky on a blind date
That's the conventional wisdom
If no one signs it out in three years it's offered for sale for fifty cents
If no one buys it it's pulped

Overkill / a protocol

page nine

red and orange that keeps beeping.
Study ties self-delusion to successful marriages.　　　　Thoughtful

　　　　　　　　pseudo-autonomies,

My inner slob

isn't talking to my outer
　　　　　　　　　　The garbage sliced

like prociutto in a situation requiring robot voices,

Three lines.
Knob on Bible and
hand on eyes.　　　　Those other words

　　　　　voice the order that hears me
　　　　　　　inside the syllabics.

Atlas proves useless.

Button pushed, weather on melt and blink

The new Carroll Gardens Sublime like about to enter a wormhole

Knows who recorded what when and can sing it

Is there nothing this bull market can't do?

The brightest light

with eyes closed

The fridge placed, an extremely coherent

family collage on bedroom wall.   Figures

page eight

The autobiographical hologram

intervenes in gender registration

Transcriptional glasses
perched on puzzled premodern faciality

damned.
The hologram   wishes to speak to the adolescent

in the cul-de-sac.

                        You will wish you'd ended here.

Another surge of Canadian air
                under Dumbo.

Voices
                        ordering me around

Eyes on Bible and hand on the knob

If I can see the poet across the street
barely wave in a dream I haven't
seen in months, then I collect

languages like curling trophies,

an agate amidst steroids.
Funny stomachs of adult development.
Those people in the corner are getting bombed

on Sean's party stuff.
A truly stupid death on ski slope.
The garbage

latent or virtual or implied.

clogged air holes, something

page four

cup moved four inches east.

About now drink something.

                    awaiting more formal procedures,
better Borg agents, 14
        or so Scottish economists, six
desiring an Apollonian
        trigger, there's that word again, the word from Porlock, the very Irishness

                of the science beyond bowling,
        smoked mozzarella, parsnips on a bed
                of unripe rhubarb

the extras mulling,

the great psychic arc,
        the syllabus.

I would leave it
to its own underground banking —

how long

has *that* pincushion
been *right* next to me? —— From which

analysis
proceeds

Myself

in the middle of an argument in which one speaker is silent

From here, this prospect,

the permutational void

avoids shape in the anti-ear

of collaborative dissonance.

They votes

page twelve

The beringed adjunct atremble in the nuttery,

just the thing for those long evenings in a tunnel

Little stabs to my herald patch.

You can tell Bach was stoned when he wrote this.

The dermatology toccata.

Insofar as it is present at the site of analysis

a countertenor will be there to inaugurate the sensorium.

You can't be sorry you wrote this, judge.

A seasonal affective disorder waiting to happen

getting fuller as the days become
stilts. Nothing in the silo

can dream itself onto the stretched surface,
the endless Eurodots of advanced composition

page five

with its teeth. And.

          Adjacent,

        the big, the bigger

bliss and sublet contingency

          a Welsh saddle of unreturnable

circuitry, *of*. Of Manx sociology,

          old guys in t-shirts.

      A plain with huts.   Friend of the army

tugged by flesh receptors. June.
      The garbage shopping of subsistence

---

bewilderment high on a list of undreamed
image, focussed on tickets
that mutate in fog of — "of" — habitual
preparation. Ten minutes later

A cop smoking to breathe
in the petunia plain, lowland
unhealth of winter juice.
7:10 next to temperature by bank.   *Into*

this charted petri dish
of ribald Archie-comicness creeps
a respondent holding sound

as though an infant, enjambed

Mayor charged in robbery. Chickens
far away slaughtered for their virus.   *Onto*
this map of recruitment dives
the championship grade sheet,

page six

filled, shirtless, a churning of tickets
to a mountain, beyond petunias
exactly one-half life size

        , the new word *thrombone*
like disease collecting in crannies
of weather, waiting.

These friends — *these*, friends —
of the uncollectible image relations,
non-nations, smoking.
Girls that happen to boys

paged at the station
Three minutes earlier.
Isosceles,
over.

Check timer.

An unreasonable cul-de-sac warmth
A cheque-cashing facility that is not of Manhattan

I notice that there is less
of what there previously had been

nubs

Gender pants dropping on deadline translated French

Vehicular swoosh,

17 23 19 versions of modernist fishing
registered by the nanotechnology

with skiers come crime and accidents.

crack bankers, bombers

page eleven

Imagine having to speak these addenda

The George Stanley sonnet ends

"Awake, and tell me there is another life!"

North of the border in a graveyard to the south
    atop a small mountain in Umbria
Sprinklers of the Okanagon desert

            A migration of insects within the body
by the shack door, an Adventist tomato
for midnight, great crates of Québequois labour

In Vietnam
her life became complicated by ladders
in histories of the Roman church,

reading *Werther* while guarding her stuff.
This is not a curriculum. Up there
            tourists are fudgies and Microsoft's browsing monopoly

            resides in the abstracted intelligence of a lizard
or a bee. A talking cure
leads geezer to construct pediment

for concrete frog.
The undrinkability
of gene-pool fluids

complicating the local cherries.
This is a spine chisel and be careful how you hold it.
            In combination, the huge toads that troubled Werther

            and the postcards of paper boots
confront the quarry of supply-side migration.
Pinnochio is a real boy because he defended Jeff.

            The rest is radio silence, symptom

page thirteen

Wasps as assemblages that seek reunion

with credentialed tarantulas. The middle
distance of logged-on glamour. Telephonic
         the pills, remembered

         the unevenly risen.

If forced to continue

The testimony reveals its fractal mandate,

skinny and wearing babies.

You can tell by the logs

arranged to spell the preposition *Anselm*.

If this is meant to be a manifesto

it is insufficiently aware of its rhetorical context.

If this, in history, seeks to glamorize

the site of epistemic hysteria,

its success is partial and on the pipe.

Guesses are shafts that call back

the cousins.

A crack in the first presocratic daybook
bending over to observe a vegetable.
Abandoned to sleep, the diabetic stanzas

reappear in the planning for centuries
of fermentation, wanting to add that
to the world as understood in a series

Page seven

Tracking shot of tended plot, fenced,
     destructive adolescents who breech its perimeter

are in us.

the magic glasses

of Joseph Smith, the made nature and Mormon certitude

of sneezes,
                I could sit staring
          at these emerging life forms far

ballroom   damnation   hologram   *there*

numberless
adjectival
transformations

       The intervention of zero
on the homiletic incline

barking oofs into history

undiscovered perimeters entirely registered as transcript technology.

That's what pays us   The latter-day
                    sanctity of little nubs, these jugs

Go way back
to the suturing of crane heat.

If this is not a seasonable disorder
it is nanocircumcision,

cheque cashed,

Page sixteen

drinking on couches, millennial as subtitled exposition,

                    How much.

Page ten

                    from the industrial unconscious

the homeless sugar toddler, the trick trees

          of teleportation, ass pain.

Stomachs are late in the recorded superego.
The insult offers a hole
                    through which worms might glow

          The official archivist
of this catatonic tradition —
The buttons enter bedroom walls

          with plans to drive drunk through the uncle.

Reruns are a good idea.

Things don't go away,

not the toggle, not the cathedral, not Virginia.

Sudden absence of birdsong.

Jammed trout weeping for origin.

The premise of this redistricting

is that holy nouns require god verbs.

The oratorical studio premise

bends the neosophistic.

The thrown peach

Page one

Knuckles of January gardening

      against the rounded corners of permanent infancy

"Unwobbling yak mind."

        The bracketed

bed down, noble gas leaks

                awaiting the gaze of screens

     is a sort of protection,

parenthetic thug alert

        Neighbours open doors
        feeling tested

A simple hello

            across decades of renovation —

        paper clip still on timer's magnet.

These heroes of agriculture are themselves silt,
the tumult of ongoing wrappers

                  probing the mesh, hopping across

continent to raise money for solid images. Pause here.

The focussing of exposed fossils in oblong clearing
Traffic copter as crashing folio

        is a revision

"The worse it gets, the better"
        the laundry will remember its odyssey,

reason as trellis   is an earlier version.

Page three

Alan Sokal
        flaking the bark off, busted

in *Dragnet*, believing

        the data, clearing throat on

huge stage collapsing
Audience in profile heads

                              lifted to begin

Bach
in Giuliani time

Rimbaud dies
As Robert Moses is born, more or less

private clouds.

What do collapses of past societies teach us?

            Mayor's private
            pain becomes
            public

      opening day descending upon the dying shortstop

speaking the Expressway

                  The working poor

a huge stage
                  in the bay, beginning

the data,
                        Child tried as adult.
Code happens

                        Impossible random Giuliani,

Page fifteen

Your enemy knows no weather

and has stolen your support poles.

Reproduction shitting students

in a deciduous foreshortening of inaugural

promise

reveals the televisual

tectonics of

the weather channel:

B minus.

Truly the end of nonnarrative cloning.

Whatever tails the academy swallows,

these dusts are context defoliants.

The auditors reply in pulses.

The vouchers, having been tricked

into "ironizing their dispute with the real,"

wander marginal park land.

Early on in academic history

rhetoric declined into trope management.

           Townies gathered sticks to poke robes.

Now these futures are traded

       like snouts in Russian subway markets,

Page two

         The better worse gets

the more habitable the intentions.

                           Seizures wrap cocktails in orality.

The perception of the magnet
          in Aristotelian dreamtime.
         Elimination trogs

battle carbon dating

as wisps of money launder the object of renovation.

If you concentrate you can feel yourself dying
       in colour within images

drawn down into the waiting gaze of agriculture.   [Rodefer: "You don't have to
I'll give you dates,   concentrate!"]
coordinates. The relation

         of birds to nonproduction in neolithic economy
is speculation
         The work week

is mesh in the revision of neighbouring memory.   Too gestural.

        If lexical schemata
        drive money fossils
             reason is a noble fluid

remembering triggers almost pulled

        in the frenzy of narrative agriculture.

          Glance at auditors.

The East Tremont section of the Bronx
in the moments before a dynamite blast shakes residences
adjacent to future Expressway

Mental defence
          moving random gourd

Page fourteen

of doomed flashes. The caretaker
wobbling on inappropriate stool.
The quote transition unquote

from mythopoeic theogony to naturalistic
cosmology — the bylaws that ensued,
the traffic tickets, recruitment kiosks. Antithesis

as conceptual tool in gusts
of impersonal calculation, the first principle
that eats us, reading on the subway.

Tubes of probability argumentation
rubbed on the necks of terrified young rhetors.
An applebox of spin swallows

speaking politely but firmly to strangers
who want something. A mistake
An inhalation of window finches

Montgomery Clift attends archaic luncheon
in science high school.

Val-u-a-ble time.

Vouchers that make the real edible
utterance, up on the roof

observing the riot,

cops on ostriches swinging hams,

dreaming of suburban patios.

Blossoms, having been tricked out to die,

wait. Sap rises too early

in Latin. How is it possible

that bits of desk are lodged in the ear,

but there you go.

A E R I A L / E D G E

Integrity & Dramatic Life, Anselm Berrigan, $10

They Beat Me Over the Head with a Sack, Anselm Berrigan, $4

the julia set, Jean Donnelly, $4

Marijuana Softdrink, Buck Downs, forthcoming 2000

Metropolis 16–20, Rob Fitterman, $5

perhaps this is a rescue fantasy, Heather Fuller, $10

Sight, Lyn Hejinian and Leslie Scalapino, $12

Late July, Gretchen Johnsen, $3

Stepping Razor, A. L. Nielsen, $9

Ace, Tom Raworth, forthcoming 2000

Errata 5uite, Joan Retallack, $12

Dogs, Phyllis Rosenzweig, $5

Aerial 9: Bruce Andrews, Rod Smith, ed., $15

Aerial 8: Barrett Watten, $16

Aerial 6/7 featuring John Cage, $15

On Your Knees, Citizen: A Collection of "Prayers" for the "Public" [Schools], Rod Smith, Lee Ann Brown, and Mark Wallace, eds., $6

Cusps, Chris Stroffolino, $2.50

Nothing Happened and Besides I Wasn't There, Mark Wallace, $9.50

Orders to: AERIAL/EDGE
             P.O. Box 25642
             Washington, D.C. 20007

Add $1 postage for individual titles. Two or more titles postpaid.